A BALANCED MATHEMATICS PROGRAM INTEGRATING SCIENCE AND LANGUAGE ARTS

Unit Resource Guide
Unit 20
Looking Back at First Grade

THIRD EDITION

KENDALL/HUNT PUBLISHING COMPANY
4050 Westmark Drive   Dubuque, Iowa   52002

A TIMS® Curriculum
University of Illinois at Chicago

UIC The University of Illinois
at Chicago

The original edition was based on work supported by the National Science Foundation under grant No. MDR 9050226 and the University of Illinois at Chicago. Any opinions, findings, and conclusions or recommendations expressed in this publication are those of the author(s) and do not necessarily reflect the views of the granting agencies.

Printed in the United States of America

1 2 3 4 5 6 7 8 9 10   11 10 09 08 07

Letter Home

Looking Back at First Grade

Date: _____

Dear Family Member:

In this unit, we reflect on what we have done in math during the past year. Your child will use concepts and skills in geometry, estimation, fractions, and whole number computation. Your child's work on the problems in this unit will provide one indication of his or her progress in mathematics over the course of the year.

As the class looks back at the math concepts they learned, you can provide additional support at home by doing the following activity:

Sunday	Monday	Tuesday	Wednesday	Thursday	Friday	Saturday
	1 $\frac{1}{2}$ inch	2	3	4	5 $\frac{1}{2}$ inch	6
7	8	9	10	11	12 $1\frac{1}{2}$ inches	13
14	15	16	17 $\frac{1}{2}$ inch	18	19	20
21	22	23	24	25	26 $\frac{1}{2}$ inch	27
28	29	30	31 3 inches			

Children will use this calendar to solve problems about the rainfall during October.

- **Math Memories List.** Invite your child to recall and discuss some of the math activities he or she did during the year. Then, have your child write a numbered list of these activities, beginning each sentence with the words "I remember." Some examples follow: (1) I remember using my footprints to measure distance. (2) I remember rolling toy cars down ramps and measuring their distance. (3) I remember making buildings out of cubes. Encourage your child to draw a picture illustrating each memory.

Thank you for supporting our math activities at home.

Sincerely,

_____

Carta al hogar

Mirando al pasado del primer grado

Fecha: _____

Estimado miembro de familia:

En esta unidad, reflexionamos acerca de lo que hemos hecho en matemáticas durante el pasado año. Su hijo/a usará conceptos y habilidades de geometría, estimación, fracciones y cálculos con números enteros. El trabajo de su hijo/a en esta unidad servirá como indicación del progreso en matemáticas durante el curso del año.

Domingo	Lunes	Martes	Miércoles	Jueves	Viernes	Sábado
	1 $\frac{1}{2}$ pulgada	2	3	4	5 $\frac{1}{2}$ pulgada	6
7	8	9	10	11	12 $1\frac{1}{2}$ pulgadas	13
14	15	16	17 $\frac{1}{2}$ pulgada	18	19	20
21	22	23	24	25	26 $\frac{1}{2}$ pulgada	27
28	29	30	31 3 pulgadas			

Los niños usarán este calendario para resolver problemas acerca de la cantidad de lluvia caída durante octubre

Mientras la clase repasa los conceptos matemáticos aprendidos, usted puede dar su apoyo adicional en casa haciendo la siguiente actividad:

- **Lista de recuerdos matemáticos.** Invite a su hijo/a a que recuerde y comente algunas de las actividades matemáticas que hizo durante el año. Luego, pídale que escriba una lista numerada de estas actividades, empezando cada oración con las palabras "Yo recuerdo". Algunos ejemplos son: (1) Yo recuerdo haber usado mis huellas para medir distancias. (2) Yo recuerdo haber puesto carritos en unas rampas y haber medido las distancias. (3) Yo recuerdo haber hecho edificios con cubos. Anime a su hijo/a a hacer un dibujo de cada recuerdo.

Gracias por su apoyo de nuestras actividades matemáticas en casa.

Atentamente,

_____

Table of Contents

Unit 20
Looking Back at First Grade

Unit 20

Outline
Looking Back at First Grade

Estimated Class Sessions

4-7

Unit Summary

In this unit, teachers can assess problem-solving progress with a series of problems as students review the concepts and skills learned in first grade. A paper-and-pencil assessment is included.

Major Concept Focus

- Assessment: problem-solving strategies
- Assessment: Grade 1 concepts and skills

Pacing Suggestions

- Lesson 1 *Problem Solving* is a set of 21 problems for students to solve during four to five class sessions. Allow time for students to share their solutions.
- Lesson 2 *End-of-Year Test* is an optional paper-and-pencil assessment.

Assessment Indicators

Use the following Assessment Indicators and the *Observational Assessment Record* that follows the Background section in this unit to assess students on key ideas.

A1. Can students solve addition and subtraction problems and explain their reasoning?

A2. Can students solve multiplication and division problems and explain their reasoning?

A3. Can students identify and extend patterns?

A4. Can students use data to solve problems?

A5. Do students use math facts strategies to add (direct modeling, counting strategies, or reasoning from known facts)?

Unit Planner

	Lesson Information	**Supplies**	**Copies/ Transparencies**

Lesson 1

Problem Solving

URG Pages 16–30
SG Pages 404–415
DPP A–H

Estimated Class Sessions
4-5

Activity
Students solve problems involving length, area, volume, and time as they revisit concepts of measurement, geometry, fractions, and arithmetic that they encountered during the year.

Math Facts Strategies
DPP items B, C, D, F, and H review and provide practice with addition math facts. Item A reviews properties of 2-D shapes. Item E reviews skip counting by fives and tens. Item G provides doubling practice.

Homework
Have students complete any unfinished problems as homework.

Assessment
1. Use students' solutions and explanations to gain insight into their thinking.
2. Have students write a journal entry for their solution strategies for one of the problems.
3. Place one or more of the problems in your students' portfolios.
4. Use Assessment Indicators A1, A2, A3, A4, and A5 and the *Observational Assessment Record* to document students' abilities to solve addition, subtraction, and division problems; identify and extend patterns; use data to solve problems; and use math facts strategies.
5. Transfer appropriate documentation from the Unit 20 *Observational Assessment Record* to students' *Individual Assessment Record Sheets*.

Supplies:
• variety of manipulatives, such as pattern blocks, chain links, connecting cubes, and toothpicks per student
• 1 calculator per student

Copies/Transparencies:
• 1 copy of *100 Chart* URG Page 24 per student
• 1 transparency each of *Problem-Solving Problems 1–21* SG Pages 404–415, optional
• 1 copy of *Observational Assessment Record* URG Pages 7–8 to be used throughout this unit
• 1 copy of *Individual Assessment Record Sheet* TIG Assessment section per student, previously copied for use throughout the year

Lesson 2

End-of-Year Test

URG Pages 31–46
DPP I–J

Estimated Class Sessions
1-2

OPTIONAL LESSON

Optional Assessment
Students complete a paper-and-pencil assessment that reviews concepts learned throughout the year.

Math Facts Strategies
DPP item I reviews area and number relationships. Item J investigates days of the week on the calendar.

Supplies:
• variety of manipulatives, such as pattern blocks, chain links, connecting cubes, toothpicks, and play money
• 1 calculator per student, optional

Copies/Transparencies:
• 1 copy of *End-of-Year Test* URG Pages 38–45 per student, optional
• 1 copy of *100 Chart* URG Page 24 per student

Background
Looking Back at First Grade

This unit consists of two lessons. The first is a set of twenty-one problems that students solve during several class sessions. The second lesson is an optional paper-and-pencil assessment. In both lessons, students draw upon strategies they acquired this year for addition, subtraction, multiplication, and division.

The first lesson reviews the concepts learned throughout the year. The problems revisit the measurement variables of length, volume, area, and time. The situations presented in the problems feature key mathematical concepts, such as number sense, patterns, arithmetic operations, geometry, estimation, and fractions. Its structure is open-ended so the manner in which you present and use the problems is left to your judgment. Allow students the opportunity to share their solutions with the class.

The optional paper-and-pencil test covers a selection of skills and concepts studied during the year. It can provide additional information to help you gauge student progress and might also be used in conjunction with school or district program evaluation efforts. The test, however, is only one small piece of the rich assessment data you have collected over the year and is not intended to serve as the primary summative assessment of student progress in mathematics.

The information you gather about students' progress during the course of this unit can be used to supplement the variety of other assessment data you have collected throughout the year—the many assessment activities embedded in various units, the anecdotal records in your *Observational Assessment Records,* activities in students' portfolios, and student journal entries. Together these assessments provide a comprehensive picture of students' mathematical progress in first grade.

Some specific concepts and skills to be assessed in the first lesson are noted in the Assessment Indicators.

Observational Assessment Record

(A1) Can students solve addition and subtraction problems and explain their reasoning?

(A2) Can students solve multiplication and division problems and explain their reasoning?

(A3) Can students identify and extend patterns?

(A4) Can students use data to solve problems?

(A5) Do students use math facts strategies to add (direct modeling, counting strategies, or reasoning from known facts)?

(A6) _____

Name	A1	A2	A3	A4	A5	A6	Comments
1.							
2.							
3.							
4.							
5.							
6.							
7.							
8.							
9.							
10.							
11.							
12.							
13.							

Name	A1	A2	A3	A4	A5	A6	Comments
14.							
15.							
16.							
17.							
18.							
19.							
20.							
21.							
22.							
23.							
24.							
25.							
26.							
27.							
28.							
29.							
30.							
31.							
32.							

Unit 20

Daily Practice and Problems
Looking Back at First Grade

A DPP Menu for Unit 20

Two Daily Practice and Problems (DPP) items are included for each class session listed in the Unit Outline. A scope and sequence chart for the DPP is in the *Teacher Implementation Guide*.

Icons in the Teacher Notes column designate the subject matter of each DPP item. Each item falls into one or more of the categories listed below. A menu of the DPP items for Unit 20 follows.

N Number Sense	✖ Computation	⧗ Time	◭ Geometry
C, E, I	G	J	A, I

⁷₊₃ Math Facts Strategies	$ Money	◩ Measurement	◿ Data
B–D, F, H	G	I	C

Addition Math Facts

Students using *Math Trailblazers* are expected to demonstrate fluency with the addition and subtraction facts by the end of second grade. The DPP for this unit reviews and practices the addition math facts in Groups F (9 + 1, 9 + 2, 9 + 3, 9 + 4, 10 + 1, 10 + 2, 10 + 3, and 10 + 4) and

G (9 + 5, 9 + 6, 9 + 7, 9 + 8, 10 + 5, 10 + 6, 10 + 7, and 10 + 8). See DPP items B, D, F, and H for specific practice of these facts. For a description of the distribution of the practice and assessment of the math facts strategies in Grade 1, see the DPP Guide in Unit 11. See also the TIMS Tutor: *Math Facts* in the *Teacher Implementation Guide*.

Unit 20 Daily Practice and Problems

Students may solve the items individually, in groups, or as a class. The items may also be assigned for homework. The DPPs are also available on the Teacher Resource CD.

Student Questions	Teacher Notes

A Name That 2-D Shape

1. I have four corners and four sides that have the same length. Name that shape.

2. I have no straight sides and no corners. Name that shape.

3. I have only three corners and three sides. Name that shape.

Encourage students to make drawings if needed.

1. Square or rhombus
2. Circle
3. Triangle

B Addition Facts I

1. $9 + 1 = $ _____

2. _____ $+ 2 = 11$

3. $9 + 3 = $ _____

4. $4 + $ _____ $= 13$

5. $11 = 1 + $ _____

6. $2 + 10 = $ _____

7. $10 + $ _____ $= 13$

8. $14 = 4 + $ _____

1. 10
2. 9
3. 12
4. 9
5. 10
6. 12
7. 3
8. 10

C Animal Evens and Odds

Matthew counted animals at the zoo. He recorded his data in a table.

Animals	Tallies	Total
Monkeys	///|	3
Bears	##+	5
Lions	||	2
Giraffes	##+ ||	7
Elephants	|//|	4

1. Which animals have an even number total?

2. Which animals have an odd number total?

3. Is the total number of bears and monkeys an even or an odd number?

4. Is the total number of giraffes and elephants an even or an odd number?

1. Lions and elephants

2. Monkeys, bears, and giraffes

3. 8; Even

4. 11; Odd

(D) Addition Facts II

A. 9¢ + 5¢ = _____

B. 15¢ = 9¢ + _____

C. _____ + 7¢ = 16¢

D. 9¢ + 8¢ = _____

E. 15¢ = 5¢ + _____

F. 10¢ + 6¢ = _____

G. 7¢ + _____ = 17¢

H. _____ + 10¢ = 18¢

A. 14¢

B. 6¢

C. 9¢

D. 17¢

E. 10¢

F. 16¢

G. 10¢

H. 8¢

(E) Skip Counting

1. Start at 30. Skip count by fives to 100.

2. Start at 17. Skip count by tens to 97.

1. 30, 35, 40, 45, 50, 55, 60, 65, 70, 75, 80, 85, 90, 95, 100

2. 17, 27, 37, 47, 57, 67, 77, 87, 97

Student Questions	Teacher Notes

 Lightning Bugs

1. Larissa and Billy captured 18 lightning bugs. When they opened their bug box to release the lightning bugs, only 8 bugs flew out. How many lightning bugs are still in the box?

2. Larissa tapped on the box and 9 more bugs flew out. How many bugs are still in the box?

1. 10 lightning bugs
2. 1 lightning bug

 Franklin's Magic Doubling Machine

Franklin found a magic doubling machine. Franklin put 5¢ into the magic doubling machine and 10¢ came out!

1. If Franklin put 17¢ into the magic doubling machine, how much money should come out?

2. If Franklin put 13¢ into the machine, how much should come out?

Give students counters and ten frames as needed to solve these problems.

1. 34¢
2. 26¢

| Student Questions | Teacher Notes |

H Laps

Tyler and Parker like to swim laps in the pool. Tyler swam 10 laps. Parker swam 6 laps.

1. How many laps did Tyler and Parker swim in all?

2. How many more laps did Tyler swim than Parker?

1. 16 laps
2. 4 laps

I Area

Constance measured the area of some objects.

Objects	Area in Sq Feet
Desktop	6
Classroom Floor	400
Board	100
Overhead Projector Screen	25
Classroom Door	32

Put the objects in order, from the smallest area to the largest area.

desktop,
overhead projector screen,
classroom door,
board,
classroom floor

J **Calendar**

1. Marty went to the store to buy milk on Monday. Four days later, he ran out of milk. What day did he run out of milk?

2. Crystal bought a dozen eggs on Saturday. Her family ate all the eggs in 3 days. What day did they run out of eggs?

Lesson 1

Problem Solving

Estimated Class Sessions

4-5

Lesson Overview

Students revisit the variables of length, area, volume, and time, and in the process demonstrate their facility with problem solving, arithmetic operations, mathematical communication, and other topics and skills. Students solve a variety of problems and share their solutions with the class. Use this lesson with other assessments to help gauge students' progress over the year.

Key Content
- Assessing problem-solving strategies.

Math Facts Strategies

DPP items B, C, D, F, and H review and provide practice with addition math facts. Item A reviews properties of 2-D shapes. Item E reviews skip counting by fives and tens. Item G provides doubling practice.

Homework

Have students complete any unfinished problems as homework.

Assessment

1. Use students' solutions and explanations to gain insight into their thinking.
2. Have students write a journal entry for their solution strategies for one of the problems.
3. Place one or more of the problems in your students' portfolios.
4. Use Assessment Indicators A1, A2, A3, A4, and A5 and the *Observational Assessment Record* to document students' abilities to solve addition, subtraction, and division problems; identify and extend patterns; use data to solve problems; and use math facts strategies.
5. Transfer appropriate documentation from the Unit 20 *Observational Assessment Record* to students' *Individual Assessment Record Sheets*.

Materials List

Supplies and Copies

Student	Teacher
Supplies for Each Student • variety of manipulatives such as pattern blocks, chain links, connecting cubes, and toothpicks • calculator	**Supplies**
Copies • 1 copy of *100 Chart* per student (*Unit Resource Guide* Page 24)	**Copies/Transparencies** • 1 transparency of *Problem-Solving Problems 1–21,* optional (*Student Guide* Pages 404–415)

All blackline masters including assessment, transparency, and DPP masters are also on the Teacher Resource CD.

Student Books
Problem-Solving Problems 1–21 (*Student Guide* Pages 404–415)

Daily Practice and Problems
DPP items A–H (*Unit Resource Guide* Pages 10–14)

Assessment Tools
Observational Assessment Record (*Unit Resource Guide* Pages 7–8)
Individual Assessment Record Sheet (*Teacher Implementation Guide,* Assessment section)

Daily Practice and Problems

Suggestions for using the DPPs are on page 22.

A. Name That 2-D Shape (URG p. 10)

1. I have four corners and four sides that have the same length. Name that shape.
2. I have no straight sides and no corners. Name that shape.
3. I have only three corners and three sides. Name that shape.

B. Addition Facts I (URG p. 10)

1. $9 + 1 = \underline{\hspace{1em}}$
2. $\underline{\hspace{1em}} + 2 = 11$
3. $9 + 3 = \underline{\hspace{1em}}$
4. $4 + \underline{\hspace{1em}} = 13$
5. $11 = 1 + \underline{\hspace{1em}}$
6. $2 + 10 = \underline{\hspace{1em}}$
7. $10 + \underline{\hspace{1em}} = 13$
8. $14 = 4 + \underline{\hspace{1em}}$

C. Animal Evens and Odds (URG p. 11)

Matthew counted animals at the zoo. He recorded his data in a table.

Animals	Tallies	Total
Monkeys	///	3
Bears	₩	5
Lions	||	2
Giraffes	₩ ||	7
Elephants	|//|	4

1. Which animals have an even number total?
2. Which animals have an odd number total?
3. Is the total number of bears and monkeys an even or an odd number?
4. Is the total number of giraffes and elephants an even or an odd number?

D. Addition Facts II (URG p. 12)

A. $9¢ + 5¢ = \underline{\hspace{1em}}$
B. $15¢ = 9¢ + \underline{\hspace{1em}}$
C. $\underline{\hspace{1em}} + 7¢ = 16¢$
D. $9¢ + 8¢ = \underline{\hspace{1em}}$
E. $15¢ = 5¢ + \underline{\hspace{1em}}$
F. $10¢ + 6¢ = \underline{\hspace{1em}}$
G. $7¢ + \underline{\hspace{1em}} = 17¢$
H. $\underline{\hspace{1em}} + 10¢ = 18¢$

E. Skip Counting (URG p. 12)

1. Start at 30. Skip count by fives to 100.
2. Start at 17. Skip count by tens to 97.

F. Lightning Bugs (URG p. 13)

1. Larissa and Billy captured 18 lightning bugs. When they opened their bug box to release the lightning bugs, only 8 bugs flew out. How many lightning bugs are still in the box?
2. Larissa tapped on the box and 9 more bugs flew out. How many bugs are still in the box?

G. Franklin's Magic Doubling Machine (URG p. 13)

Franklin found a magic doubling machine. Franklin put 5¢ into the magic doubling machine and 10¢ came out!

1. If Franklin put 17¢ into the magic doubling machine, how much money should come out?
2. If Franklin put 13¢ into the machine, how much should come out?

H. Laps (URG p. 14)

Tyler and Parker like to swim laps in the pool. Tyler swam 10 laps. Parker swam 6 laps.

1. How many laps did Tyler and Parker swim in all?
2. How many more laps did Tyler swim than Parker?

Teaching the Activity

Invite students to think about and discuss some of the activities they completed during the year. To trigger their memories, mention activities involving previous work with measurement concepts:

- Measuring distances using footprints
- Measuring the distance traveled by a toy car rolling down a ramp
- Measuring distances between objects plotted on a left/right map
- Measuring the volume of containers using different sizes of beans
- Measuring the area of three rectangles in square inches, based on a variation of the tale "Goldilocks and the Three Bears"

Remind students of their experiences constructing buildings with cubes and using calendars to explore time. Guide the class discussion by focusing on four measurement variables—length, area, volume, and time—to introduce the *Problem-Solving Problems 1–21* Activity Pages.

To help students get started, display a transparency of one of the problems from the *Problem-Solving Problems 1–21* Activity Pages. As students solve the problem, make sure they are aware of the tools—pattern blocks, chain links, connecting cubes, toothpicks, *100 Charts,* and calculators—that are available for their use. Then invite students to share their answers and solutions with the class.

Students can work on the remaining problems individually, in pairs, or in small groups. You may choose to have the entire class work simultaneously on the same problem or have half the class work on one problem while the other half works on another. In either case, invite students to share their solutions with the class. You may find that students will solve only two or three problems each session.

Name _____ Date _____

Problem-Solving Problems 1–21

Problem 1

Complete the following part-part-whole problems. Write a number sentence for each one.

Part	Part
5	3
Whole	

Part	Part
50	
Whole	
80	

Part	Part
	300
Whole	
800	

_____   _____   _____

Problem 2

Pretend you have measured the following objects. Write the names of the objects in the proper column below.

clock 24 links   window 86 links   bookcase 95 links   door 72 links   table 38 links

0–25 links	26–50 links	51–75 links	76–100 links

SG • Grade 1 • Unit 20 • Lesson 1   Problem Solving

Student Guide - **page 404** *(Answers on p. 25)*

Name _____ Date _____

Problem 3

Write the number that each drawing of beans represents.

10 10 10   _____

100 10 10   _____

50 10 10   _____

Problem 4

Draw a picture for this story. Solve the problem.

Alex had 15 marbles. Seven of them rolled under the stairs. How many marbles did he have then?

Problem Solving   SG • Grade 1 • Unit 20 • Lesson 1

Student Guide - **page 405** *(Answers on p. 25)*

URG • Grade 1 • Unit 20 • Lesson 1   **19**

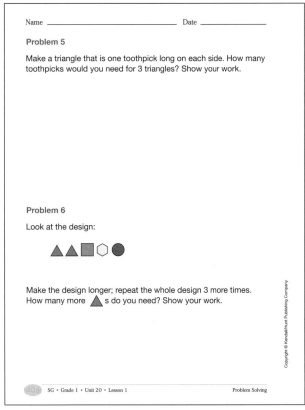

Student Guide - page 406 (Answers on p. 26)

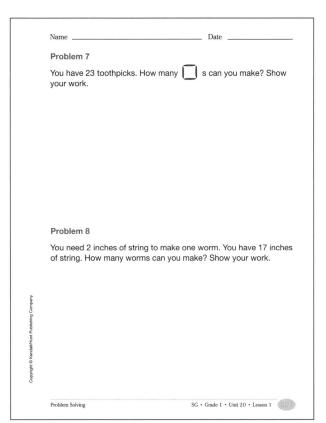

Student Guide - page 407 (Answers on p. 26)

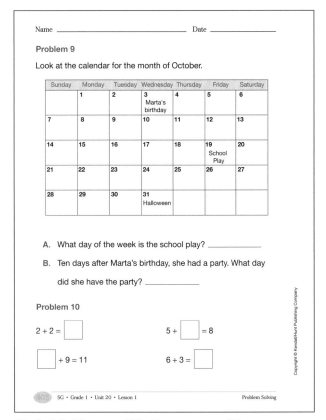

Student Guide - page 408 (Answers on p. 27)

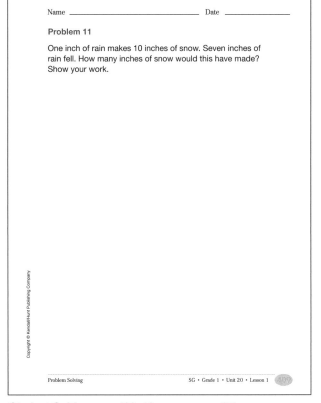

Student Guide - page 409 (Answers on p. 27)

Name _____ Date _____

Problem 12

Juan uses $5\frac{1}{2}$ square inches of paper to cover a shape. Marta uses $7\frac{1}{2}$ square inches of paper to cover another shape. How many more square inches of paper does Marta use?

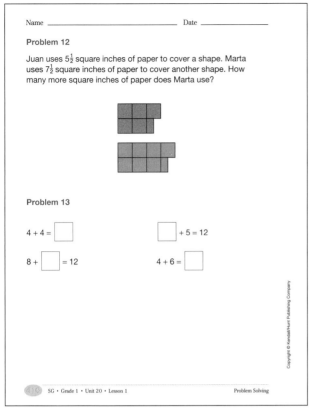

Problem 13

$4 + 4 =$ ☐   ☐ $+ 5 = 12$

$8 +$ ☐ $= 12$ $4 + 6 =$ ☐

Student Guide - page 410 *(Answers on p. 28)*

Name _____ Date _____

Problem 14

Draw the missing shape.

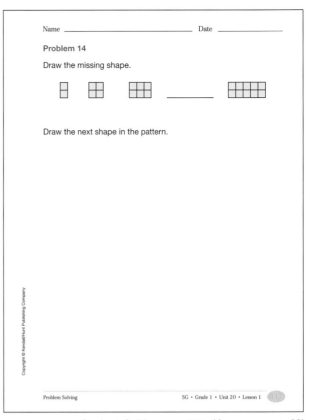

Draw the next shape in the pattern.

Student Guide - page 411 *(Answers on p. 28)*

Name _____ Date _____

Problem 15

Georgina made a building. She used:
- 12 cubes on the first floor
- 8 cubes on the second floor
- 2 cubes on the third floor
- 1 cube on the top

How many cubes did she use altogether? Show your work.

Problem 16

You find a pile of 53 cubes. How many 8-cube buildings can you make? Show your work.

Student Guide - page 412 *(Answers on p. 29)*

Name _____ Date _____

Problem 17

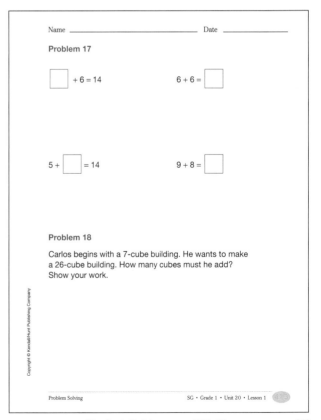

☐ $+ 6 = 14$ $6 + 6 =$ ☐

$5 +$ ☐ $= 14$ $9 + 8 =$ ☐

Problem 18

Carlos begins with a 7-cube building. He wants to make a 26-cube building. How many cubes must he add? Show your work.

Student Guide - page 413 *(Answers on p. 29)*

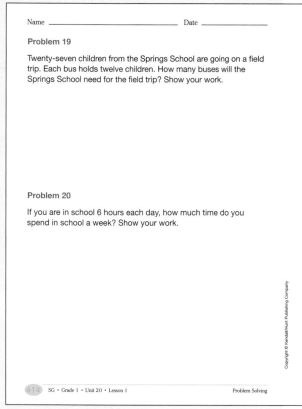

Name _____ Date _____

Problem 19

Twenty-seven children from the Springs School are going on a field trip. Each bus holds twelve children. How many buses will the Springs School need for the field trip? Show your work.

Problem 20

If you are in school 6 hours each day, how much time do you spend in school a week? Show your work.

SG • Grade 1 • Unit 20 • Lesson 1   Problem Solving

Student Guide - page 414 *(Answers on p. 30)*

Name _____ Date _____

Problem 21

$10 + 9 = \boxed{}$

$\boxed{} + 10 = 16$

$3 + \boxed{} = 13$

$9 + 3 = \boxed{}$

Problem Solving   SG • Grade 1 • Unit 20 • Lesson 1

Student Guide - page 415 *(Answers on p. 30)*

Math Facts Strategies

DPP item B provides practice with the addition math facts in Group F. Item C reviews math facts using data in a table to solve problems. Item D provides practice with the addition math facts in Group G. Items F and H review math facts in a series of word problems.

Homework and Practice

- Assign as homework any problems that were not completed in class.
- DPP item A reviews two-dimensional shapes. Item E reviews skip counting and item G reviews doubling.

Assessment

- This unit offers opportunities to gain insight into the thinking of your students. Look for the following:
  - Children who understand the elements of the problem and their relationships to one another.
  - Children who can explain the problem's mathematical concepts.
  - Children who offer complete and clear responses.
- Have students write a journal entry for their solution strategies for one of the problems. This writing can serve as an assessment of their mathematical communication skills.
- Place one or more of the problems in your students' portfolios. This is a good opportunity to review your students' portfolios with them.
- Use the *Observational Assessment Record* to document students' abilities to solve addition, subtraction, multiplication, and division problems and explain their strategies; identify and extend patterns; use data to solve problems; and use math facts strategies.
- Transfer appropriate assessment documentation from the Unit 20 *Observational Assessment Record* to students' *Individual Assessment Record Sheets*.

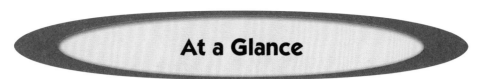

Estimated Class Sessions **4-5**

At a Glance

Math Facts Strategies and Daily Practice and Problems

DPP items B, C, D, F, and H review and practice addition math facts. Item A reviews properties of 2-D shapes. Item E reviews skip counting by fives and tens. Item G practices doubling.

Teaching the Activity (A1) (A2) (A3) (A4) (A5)

1. Over a period of several days, students complete *Problem-Solving Problems 1–21*.
2. Students share their thinking and solution strategies for various problems with the class.

Homework

Have students complete any unfinished problems as homework.

Assessment

1. Use students' solutions and explanations to gain insight into their thinking.
2. Have students write a journal entry for their solution strategies for one of the problems.
3. Place one or more of the problems in your students' portfolios.
4. Use Assessment Indicators A1, A2, A3, A4, and A5 and the *Observational Assessment Record* to document students' abilities to solve addition, subtraction, and division problems; identify and extend patterns; use data to solve problems; and use math facts strategies.
5. Transfer appropriate documentation from the Unit 20 *Observational Assessment Record* to students' *Individual Assessment Record Sheets*.

Answer Key is on pages 25–30.

Notes:

URG • Grade 1 • Unit 20 • Lesson 1   **23**

100 Chart

1	2	3	4	5	6	7	8	9	10
11	12	13	14	15	16	17	18	19	20
21	22	23	24	25	26	27	28	29	30
31	32	33	34	35	36	37	38	39	40
41	42	43	44	45	46	47	48	49	50
51	52	53	54	55	56	57	58	59	60
61	62	63	64	65	66	67	68	69	70
71	72	73	74	75	76	77	78	79	80
81	82	83	84	85	86	87	88	89	90
91	92	93	94	95	96	97	98	99	100

Student Guide (p. 404)

Problem-Solving Problems 1–21

1. $5 + 3 = 8$
$50 + 30 = 80$
$500 + 300 = 800$

2.

0-25 links	26-50 links	51-75 links	76-100 links
clock	table	door	window bookcase

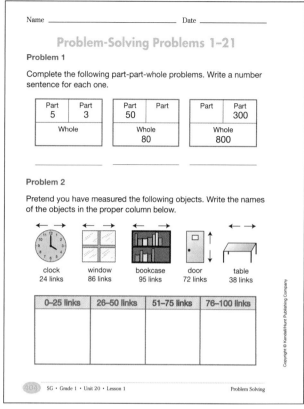

Student Guide (p. 405)

Problem-Solving Problems 1–21

3. 35; 123; 74

4. Pictures will vary. He will have 8 marbles.

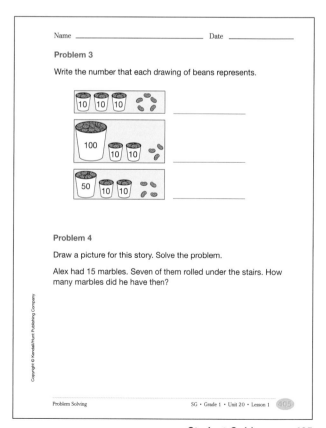

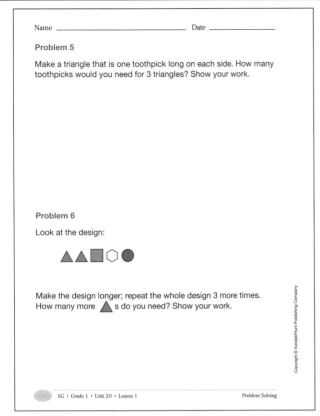

Student Guide - page 406

Student Guide (p. 406)

Problem-Solving Problems 1–21

5. 9 toothpicks

6. 6 more triangles

△ △ □ ◇ ○ △ △ □ ◇ ○ △ △ □ ◇ ○
△ △ □ ◇ ○

Student Guide (p. 407)

Problem-Solving Problems 1–21

7. 5 with 3 toothpicks left over

8. 8 worms with 1 inch of string left over
$2 + 2 + 2 + 2 + 2 + 2 + 2 + 2 + 1 = 17$

Student Guide - page 407

Student Guide (p. 408)

Problem-Solving Problems 1–21

9. **A.** Friday

   B. Saturday, October 13

10. $2 + 2 = \boxed{4}$

    $5 + \boxed{3} = 8$

    $\boxed{2} + 9 = 11$

    $6 + 3 = \boxed{9}$

Name _____ Date _____

Problem 9

Look at the calendar for the month of October.

Sunday	Monday	Tuesday	Wednesday	Thursday	Friday	Saturday
	1	2	3 Marta's birthday	4	5	6
7	8	9	10	11	12	13
14	15	16	17	18	19 School Play	20
21	22	23	24	25	26	27
28	29	30	31 Halloween			

A. What day of the week is the school play? _____

B. Ten days after Marta's birthday, she had a party. What day did she have the party? _____

Problem 10

$2 + 2 = \boxed{}$ $5 + \boxed{} = 8$

$\boxed{} + 9 = 11$ $6 + 3 = \boxed{}$

408   SG • Grade 1 • Unit 20 • Lesson 1   Problem Solving

Student Guide - page 408

Student Guide (p. 409)

Problem-Solving Problems 1–21

11. 70 inches

    $10 + 10 + 10 + 10 + 10 + 10 + 10 = 70$

Name _____ Date _____

Problem 11

One inch of rain makes 10 inches of snow. Seven inches of rain fell. How many inches of snow would this have made? Show your work.

Problem Solving   SG • Grade 1 • Unit 20 • Lesson 1   409

Student Guide - page 409

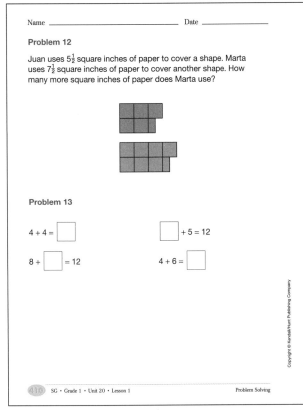

Name _____ Date _____

Problem 12

Juan uses $5\frac{1}{2}$ square inches of paper to cover a shape. Marta uses $7\frac{1}{2}$ square inches of paper to cover another shape. How many more square inches of paper does Marta use?

Problem 13

4 + 4 = ☐   ☐ + 5 = 12

8 + ☐ = 12   4 + 6 = ☐

SG • Grade 1 • Unit 20 • Lesson 1   Problem Solving

Student Guide - page 410

Student Guide (p. 410)

Problem-Solving Problems 1–21

12. 2 square inches more

13. $4 + 4 = \boxed{8}$

$\boxed{7} + 5 = 12$

$8 + \boxed{4} = 12$

$4 + 6 = \boxed{10}$

Name _____ Date _____

Problem 14

Draw the missing shape.

Draw the next shape in the pattern.

Problem Solving   SG • Grade 1 • Unit 20 • Lesson 1

Student Guide - page 411

Student Guide (p. 411)

Problem-Solving Problems 1–21

14. missing shape   next shape

 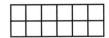

Student Guide (p. 412)

Problem-Solving Problems 1–21

15. $12 + 8 + 2 + 1 = 23$ cubes

16. 6 buildings with 5 cubes left over
   $8 + 8 + 8 + 8 + 8 + 8 + 5 = 53$

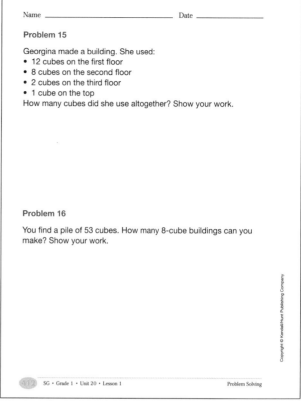

Name _____ Date _____

Problem 15

Georgina made a building. She used:
- 12 cubes on the first floor
- 8 cubes on the second floor
- 2 cubes on the third floor
- 1 cube on the top

How many cubes did she use altogether? Show your work.

Problem 16

You find a pile of 53 cubes. How many 8-cube buildings can you make? Show your work.

SG • Grade 1 • Unit 20 • Lesson 1   Problem Solving

Student Guide - page 412

Student Guide (p. 413)

Problem-Solving Problems 1–21

17. $\boxed{8} + 6 = 14$

   $6 + 6 = \boxed{12}$

   $5 + \boxed{9} = 14$

   $9 + 8 = \boxed{17}$

18. 19 cubes; $7 + 19 = 26$

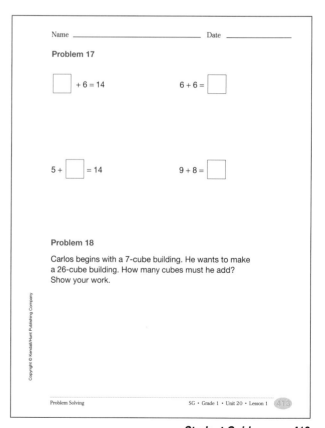

Name _____ Date _____

Problem 17

$\boxed{} + 6 = 14$ $6 + 6 = \boxed{}$

$5 + \boxed{} = 14$ $9 + 8 = \boxed{}$

Problem 18

Carlos begins with a 7-cube building. He wants to make a 26-cube building. How many cubes must he add? Show your work.

Problem Solving   SG • Grade 1 • Unit 20 • Lesson 1

Student Guide - page 413

Student Guide - page 414

Student Guide - page 415

Student Guide (p. 414)

Problem-Solving Problems 1–21

19. 3 buses; $12 + 12 + 3 = 27$

20. 30 hours; $6 + 6 + 6 + 6 + 6 = 30$

Student Guide (p. 415)

Problem-Solving Problems 1–21

21. $10 + 9 = \boxed{19}$

$\boxed{6} + 10 = 16$

$3 + \boxed{10} = 13$

$9 + 3 = \boxed{12}$

End-of-Year Test

Lesson Overview

Estimated Class Sessions
1-2

This optional paper-and-pencil test is for teachers who wish to have this type of assessment, in conjunction with others, to help gauge students' progress over the course of the year. Though the test does not cover all the concepts and skills studied during the year, it can serve as one way of communicating to second grade teachers the kinds of mathematics experienced by first grade students.

Key Content

- Assessing problem-solving strategies and concepts.

Math Facts Strategies

DPP item I reviews area and number relationships. Item J investigates days of the week on the calendar.

Materials List

Supplies and Copies

Student	Teacher
Supplies for Each Student • variety of manipulatives such as pattern blocks, chain links, connecting cubes, toothpicks, and play money • calculator, optional	**Supplies**
Copies • 1 copy of *End-of-Year Test* per student, optional (*Unit Resource Guide* Pages 38–45) • 1 copy of *100 Chart* per student (*Unit Resource Guide* Page 24)	**Copies/Transparencies**

All blackline masters including assessment, transparency, and DPP masters are also on the Teacher Resource CD.

Daily Practice and Problems

DPP items I–J (*Unit Resource Guide* Pages 14–15)

Daily Practice and Problems

Suggestions for using the DPPs are on page 37.

I. Area (URG p. 14)

Constance measured the area of some objects.

Objects	Area in Sq Feet
Desktop	6
Classroom Floor	400
Board	100
Overhead Projector Screen	25
Classroom Door	32

Put the objects in order, from the smallest area to the largest area.

J. Calendar (URG p. 15)

1. Marty went to the store to buy milk on Monday. Four days later, he ran out of milk. What day did he run out of milk?
2. Crystal bought a dozen eggs on Saturday. Her family ate all the eggs in 3 days. What day did they run out of eggs?

Unit Resource Guide - page 38

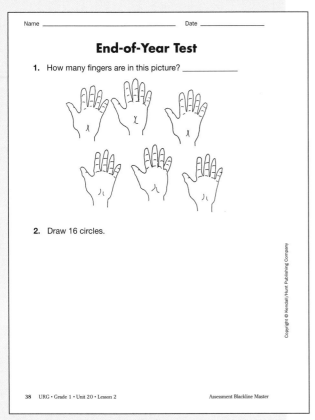

Name _____ Date _____

End-of-Year Test

1. How many fingers are in this picture? _____

2. Draw 16 circles.

38   URG • Grade 1 • Unit 20 • Lesson 2   Assessment Blackline Master

Unit Resource Guide - page 38

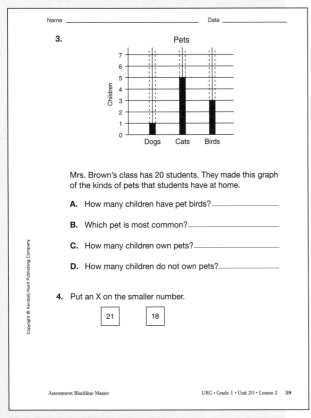

Name _____ Date _____

3.

Pets

Mrs. Brown's class has 20 students. They made this graph of the kinds of pets that students have at home.

A. How many children have pet birds? _____

B. Which pet is most common? _____

C. How many children own pets? _____

D. How many children do not own pets? _____

4. Put an X on the smaller number.

| 21 | | 18 |

Assessment Blackline Master   URG • Grade 1 • Unit 20 • Lesson 2   39

Unit Resource Guide - page 39

Teaching the Assessment

This assessment activity can be completed in a variety of ways. Use it in any manner that fits your classroom or school needs. Manipulatives and *100 Charts* should be available for student use. This assessment can be completed independently or in groups.

Encourage students to give full answers for each of the questions. They can draw pictures or write their solutions in words.

Questions 1–23 Explanations and answers.

1. 30 fingers; students may count by ones or use skip counting strategies with groups of tens or fives.

2. Students should show 16 circles.

3. a. 3 children
    b. cats
    c. 9 children; 1 + 5 + 3 = 9 children
    d. 11 children

4. Students should mark the box with 18.

For *Questions 5* and *6* tell students to show how they solved the problems. They may use counters and write their solutions in words or draw a picture to illustrate the problem. Some students may choose to show an addition or subtraction number sentence.

5. 3 pockets; 7 − 4 = 3 or 3 + 4 = 7

6. 6 cookies

7. Joe would have 19 trolls. At this point in the first grade year, some students will be able to quickly identify and use the appropriate addition fact to solve this problem. Encourage them to either draw a picture or write a number sentence to show how they arrived at their answer.

8. Students should select all three-sided figures regardless of their orientation.

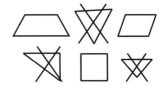

34   URG • Grade 1 • Unit 20 • Lesson 2

Name _____ Date _____

5. A boy has 4 pockets on his pants. He has some pockets on his shirt. He has 7 pockets in all. How many pockets are on his shirt? Show your work.

Number of pockets _____

6. If you had 12 cookies and shared them evenly with your friend, how many cookies would your friend get? Show your work.

Unit Resource Guide - page 40

Name _____ Date _____

7. Joe had 13 trolls. If he got 6 more trolls, how many would he have? Show your work.

_____

8. Put an X on all the triangles.

9. Put an X on all the squares below.

Unit Resource Guide - page 41

---

9. To answer this question, students need to understand that a square has 4 equal sides and 4 right angles. A shape with 4 right angles and 4 equal sides remains a square regardless of orientation.

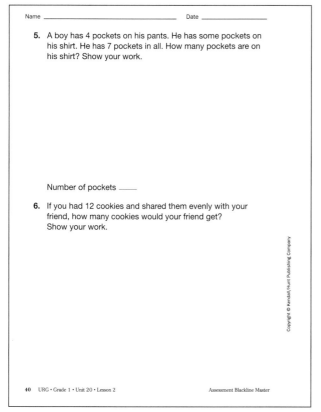

10. There are 63 dots in all.

For **Questions 11–14** the completed sequences are:

11. 7, 8, 9, 10, 11, 12 (counting by ones)
12. 20, 30, 40, 50, 60, 70 (counting by tens)
13. 5, 10, 15, 20, 25, 30 (counting by fives)
14. 11, 16, 21, 26, 31, 36 (counting by fives starting with 11)

Name _____ Date _____

10. Write how many dots there are in all. _____

Fill in the blanks by following the pattern:

11. 7, 8, 9, ____, ____, ____

12. 20, 30, 40, ____, ____, ____

13. 5, 10, 15, ____, ____, ____

14. 11, 16, 21, ____, ____, ____

Unit Resource Guide - page 42

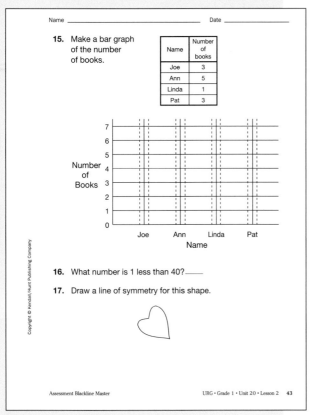

Unit Resource Guide - page 43

15.

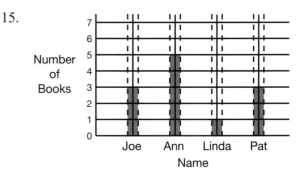

16. 39; students should be able to solve this by counting back from 40. However, some may choose to write a subtraction number sentence $40 - 1 = 39$ or an addition number sentence $39 + 1 = 40$.

17. Students should draw the line that would allow the heart to be folded in half.

18. 7 sq in; students' answers should include the unit of measurement.

19. Students may color any one of the four sections.

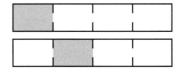

20. 9, 17, 23, 51

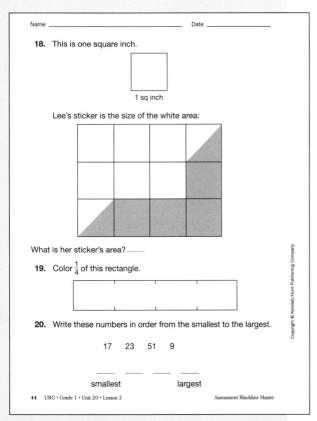

Unit Resource Guide - page 44

In the candy store problems, students must use all the information given about the problems, both in the question and in the illustration and narrative. Students may use play money to help them solve these problems.

21. 7; $2 + 2 + 2 + 2 + 2 + 2 + 2 = 14$. Since Bob has fifteen cents, he does not have enough money to pay for an eighth orange candy.

22. 1¢; since Bob bought seven orange candies that cost 2¢ each, he had 1¢ left. If students did not answer *Question 21* correctly, you may have to decide whether you want to allow partial credit for an answer here that shows correct calculation using the student's answer in *Question 21.*

23. 1 yellow and 1 red; $10¢ + 5¢ = 15¢$. Here, even though Bob may want to buy orange candies, if he is going to spend all his money on two candies, he has to buy the yellow and red.

You may wish to have students share their solutions and solution strategies.

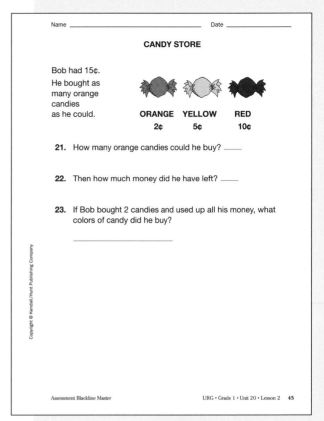

Unit Resource Guide - page 45

Math Facts Strategies and Daily Practice and Problems

DPP item I reviews area and number relationships. Item J investigates days of the week on the calendar.

Teaching the Assessment (A1) (A2) (A3) (A4) (A5)

1. Students complete the *End-of-Year Test* Assessment Pages.
2. On the following day, students share their solutions and solution strategies.

Answer Key is on page 46.

Notes:

End-of-Year Test

1. How many fingers are in this picture? _____

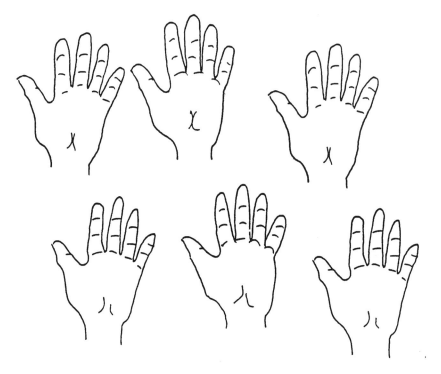

2. Draw 16 circles.

3.

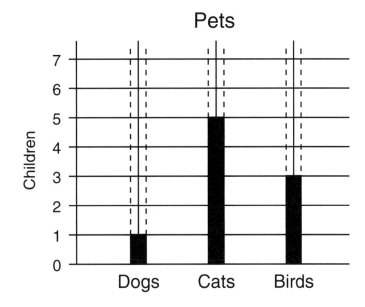

Mrs. Brown's class has 20 students. They made this graph of the kinds of pets that students have at home.

A. How many children have pet birds?_____

B. Which pet is most common?_____

C. How many children own pets?_____

D. How many children do not own pets?_____

4. Put an X on the smaller number.

| 21 | | 18 |

5. A boy has 4 pockets on his pants. He has some pockets on his shirt. He has 7 pockets in all. How many pockets are on his shirt? Show your work.

Number of pockets _____

6. If you had 12 cookies and shared them evenly with your friend, how many cookies would your friend get?
Show your work.

Assessment Blackline Master

7. Joe had 13 trolls. If he got 6 more trolls, how many would he have? Show your work.

_____

8. Put an X on all the triangles.

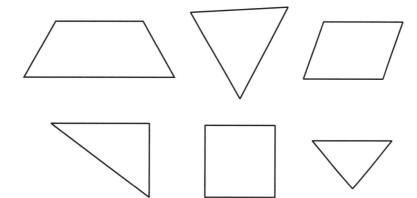

9. Put an X on all the squares below.

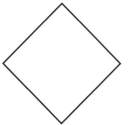

10. Write how many dots there are in all. _____

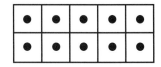 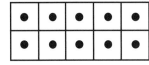 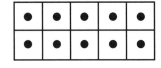

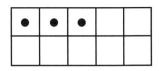

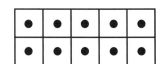 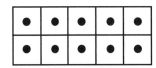 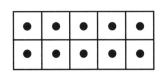

Fill in the blanks by following the pattern:

11. 7, 8, 9, ____, ____, ____

12. 20, 30, 40, ____, ____, ____

13. 5, 10, 15, ____, ____, ____

14. 11, 16, 21, ____, ____, ____

Assessment Blackline Master

15. Make a bar graph
of the number
of books.

Name	Number of books
Joe	3
Ann	5
Linda	1
Pat	3

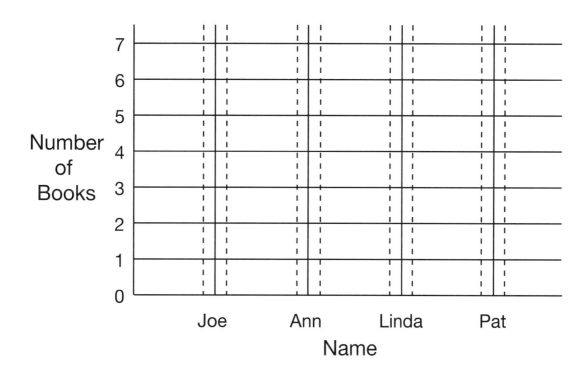

Number
of
Books

7
6
5
4
3
2
1
0

Joe   Ann   Linda   Pat

Name

16. What number is 1 less than 40? _____

17. Draw a line of symmetry for this shape.

18. This is one square inch.

1 sq inch

Lee's sticker is the size of the white area:

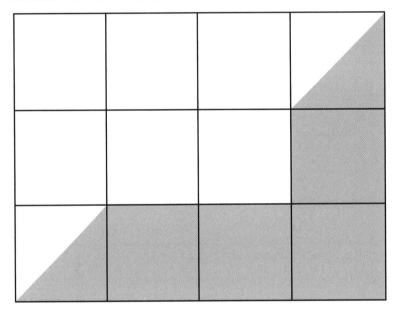

What is her sticker's area? _____

19. Color $\frac{1}{4}$ of this rectangle.

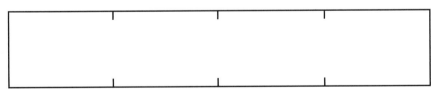

20. Write these numbers in order from the smallest to the largest.

17   23   51   9

_____ _____ _____ _____

smallest   largest

Copyright © Kendall/Hunt Publishing Company

CANDY STORE

Bob had 15¢.

He bought as
many orange
candies
as he could.

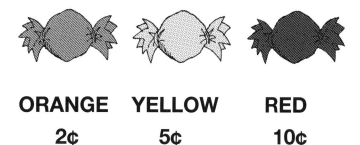

ORANGE   **YELLOW**   **RED**

2¢   5¢   10¢

21. How many orange candies could he buy? _____

22. Then how much money did he have left? _____

23. If Bob bought 2 candies and used up all his money, what colors of candy did he buy?

_____

Unit Resource Guide (pp. 38–45)

End-of-Year Test

See Lesson Guide 2 for all the answers.*

*Answers and/or discussion are included in the Lesson Guide.

Glossary

This glossary provides definitions of key vocabulary terms in the Grade 1 lessons. Locations of key vocabulary terms in the curriculum are included with each definition. Components Key: URG = *Unit Resource Guide* and SG = *Student Guide.*

A

Approximate (URG Unit 12)
1. (adjective) a number that is close to the desired number
2. (verb) to estimate

Area (URG Unit 10; SG Unit 12)
The amount of space that a shape covers. Area is measured in square units.

B

C

Capacity (URG Unit 9)
1. The volume of the inside of a container.
2. The largest volume a container can hold.

Circle (URG Unit 2)
A curve that is made up of all the points that are the same distance from one point, the center.

Circumference (URG Unit 15)
The distance around a circle.

Coordinates (URG Unit 19)
(In the plane) Two numbers that specify the location of a point on a flat surface relative to a reference point called the origin. The two numbers are the distances from the point to two perpendicular lines called axes.

Counting All (URG Unit 1)
A strategy for adding in which students start at one and count until the total is reached.

Counting Back (URG Unit 8)
A method of subtraction that involves counting from the larger number to the smaller one. For example, to find 8 − 5 the student counts 7, 6, 5 which is 3 less.

Counting On (URG Unit 1 & Unit 4)
A strategy for adding two numbers in which students start with one of the numbers and then count until the total is reached. For example, to count 6 + 3, begin with 6 and count three more, 7, 8, 9.

Counting Up (URG Unit 8)
A method of subtraction that involves counting from the smaller number to the larger one. For example, to find 8 − 5 the student counts 6, 7, 8 which is 3 more.

Cube (URG Unit 12 & Unit 15)
A solid with six congruent square faces.

Cubic Units (URG Unit 12)
A unit for measuring volume— a cube that measures one unit along each edge. For example, cubic centimeters and cubic inches.

cubic centimeter

Cylinder (URG Unit 15)
A three-dimensional figure with two parallel congruent circles as bases (top and bottom) and a curved side that is the union of parallel lines connecting corresponding points on the circles.

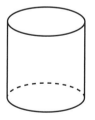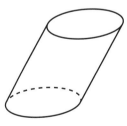

D

Data Table (URG Unit 3)
A tool for recording and organizing data on paper or on a computer.

Name	Age

Division by Measuring Out (URG Unit 14)
A type of division problem in which the number in each group is known and the unknown is the number of groups. For example, twenty students are divided into teams of four students each. How many teams are there? (20 students ÷ 4 students per team = 5 teams) This type of division is also known as measurement division.

Division by Sharing (URG Unit 14)
A type of division problem in which the number of groups is known and the unknown is the number in each group. For example, twenty students are divided into five teams. How many students are on each team? (20 students ÷ 5 teams = 4 students per team) This type of division is also known as partitive division.

E

Edge (URG Unit 15)
A line segment where two faces of a three-dimensional figure meet.

Equivalent Fractions (URG Unit 18)
Two fractions are equivalent if they represent the same part of the whole. For example, if a class has 8 boys and 8 girls, we can say $\frac{8}{16}$ of the students are girls or $\frac{1}{2}$ of the students are girls.

Even Number (URG Unit 4 & Unit 13)
Numbers that are doubles. The numbers 0, 2, 4, 6, 8, 10, etc. are even. The number 28 is even because it is 14 + 14.

F

Face (URG Unit 12 & Unit 15)
A flat side of a three-dimensional figure.

Fixed Variables (URG Unit 2, Unit 6 & Unit 11)
Variables in an experiment that are held constant or not changed. These variables are often called controlled variables.

G

H

Hexagon (URG Unit 2)
A six-sided polygon.

I

J

K

L

Length (URG Unit 6 & Unit 10)
1. The distance along a line or curve from one point to another. Distance can be measured with a ruler or tape measure.
2. The distance from one "end" to another of a two- or three-dimensional figure. For example, the length of a rectangle usually refers to the length of the longer side.

Line
A set of points that form a straight path extending infinitely in two directions.

Line Symmetry (URG Unit 7 & Unit 18)
A figure has line symmetry if it can be folded along a line so that the two halves match exactly.

Line of Symmetry (URG Unit 7 & Unit 18)
A line such that if a figure is folded along the line, then one half of the figure matches the other.

M

Making a Ten (URG Unit 13)
A strategy for adding and subtracting that takes advantage of students' knowledge of partitions of ten. For example, a student might find 8 + 4 by breaking the 4 into 2 + 2 and then using a knowledge of sums that add to ten.

$$8 + 4 =$$
$$8 + 2 + 2 =$$
$$10 + 2 = 12$$

Median (URG Unit 6 & Unit 9)
The number "in the middle" of a set of data. If there is an odd number of data, it is the number in the middle when the numbers are arranged in order. So the median of {1, 2, 14, 15, 28, 29, 30} is 15. If there is an even number of data, it is the number halfway between the two middle numbers. The median of {1, 2, 14, 15, 28, 29} is $14\frac{1}{2}$.

Mr. Origin (URG Unit 19)
A plastic figure used to help childen learn about direction and distance.

N

Near Double (URG Unit 13)
A derived addition or subtraction fact found by using doubles. For example, 3 + 4 = 7 follows from the fact that 3 + 3 = 6.

Number Sentence (URG Unit 3 & Unit 4)
A number sentence uses numbers and symbols instead of words to describe a problem. For example, a number sentence for the problem "5 birds landed on a branch. Two more birds also landed on the branch. How many birds are on the branch?" is 5 + 2 = 7.

O

Odd Number (URG Unit 4)
A number that is not even. The odd numbers are 1, 3, 5, 7, 9, and so on.

Origin (URG Unit 19)
A reference point for a coordinate system. If the coordinate system is a line, we can determine the location of an object on the line by the number of units it is to the right or the left of the origin.

P

Part (URG Unit 4)
One of the addends in part-part-whole addition problems.

Pattern Unit (URG Unit 7)
The portion of a pattern that is repeated. For example, AAB is the pattern unit in the pattern AABAABAAB.

Perimeter (URG Unit 6; SG Unit 12)
The distance around a two-dimensional shape.

Polygon
A closed, connected plane figure consisting of line segments, with exactly two segments meeting at each end point.

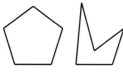 

Polygons   Not Polygons

Prediction (URG Unit 5)
Using a sample to predict what is likely to occur in the population.

Prism (URG Unit 15)
A solid that has two congruent and parallel bases. The remaining faces (sides) are parallelograms. A rectangular prism has bases that are rectangles. A box is a common object that is shaped like a rectangular prism.

Q

Quadrilateral
A polygon with four sides.

R

Rectangle (URG Unit 2)
A quadrilateral with four right angles.

Rhombus (URG Unit 2)
A quadrilateral with four sides of equal length.

Rotational Symmetry (URG Unit 7)
A figure has rotational (or turn) symmetry if there is a point on the figure and a rotation of less than 360° about that point so that it "fits" on itself. For example, a square has a turn symmetry of $\frac{1}{4}$ turn (or 90°) about its center.

S

Sample (URG Unit 5)
Some of the items from a whole group.

Sphere (URG Unit 15)
A three-dimensional figure that is made up of points that are the same distance from one point, the center. A basketball is a common object shaped like a sphere.

Square (URG Unit 2)
A polygon with four equal sides and four right angles.

Symmetry (URG Unit 18)
(See Line Symmetry, Line of Symmetry, and Rotational Symmetry.)

T

Three-dimensional Shapes (URG Unit 15)
A figure in space that has length, width, and height.

TIMS Laboratory Method (URG Unit 5)
A method that students use to organize experiments and investigations. It involves four components: draw, collect, graph, and explore. It is a way to help students learn about the scientific method. TIMS is an acronym for Teaching Integrated Mathematics and Science.

Trapezoid (URG Unit 2)
A quadrilateral with exactly one pair of parallel sides.

Trial (URG Unit 6)
One attempt in an experiment.

Triangle (URG Unit 2)
A polygon with three sides.

Turn Symmetry
(See Rotational Symmetry.)

U

Using Doubles (URG Unit 13)
A strategy for adding and subtracting which uses derived facts from known doubles. For example, students use 7 + 7 = 14 to find that 7 + 8 is one more or 15.

Using Ten (URG Unit 13)
A strategy for adding which uses reasoning from known facts. For example, students use 3 + 7 = 10 to find that 4 + 7 is one more or 11.

V

Variable (URG Unit 2 & Unit 11)
A variable is something that varies or changes in an experiment.

Volume (URG Unit 9 & Unit 12;
   SG Unit 12)
1. The amount of space an object takes up.
2. The amount of space inside a container.

W

Whole (URG Unit 4)
The sum in part-part-whole addition problems.

X

Y

Z